SPILLING THE TEA!

*A guide to leaning in on your life,
removing the pain, and living free.*

LADY B

DEDICATION

I dedicate this book to my mother. You passed when I was 6, but your spirit lives in me. Thank you for being the vessel chosen for my existence. Looking into your lineage, you came from pain, abuse, neglect, and brokenness. Your love is so strong it called for me to heal, and share my healing with the world. I am sorry for the pain you endured. May all the generational curses stop here. I love you momma.

To all those parentless children, even those who are now adults, please know, God doesn't make mistakes, he creates gifts. There is a treasure in you. I pray you have the courage to heal and live your gifts. The world needs you.

Here are some reviews from clients who were excited to share their experience with my services and T therapy. I picked only a few so that this didn't become a book of reviews, but I feel it is important you are able to hear from my clients directly regarding their results. They were asked the following questions:

1. What was the major concern or reason that brought you to me for my services?
2. What T therapy did for you?
3. Why would you recommend my services?
4. What has working with me done for you?
5. Is T therapy something you can always get use out of? Will you continue to use it?

A. Phillips, California.

I had lost a good amount of weight and size, had plastic surgery but still felt so empty. I felt out of control of my emotions and myself. Fighting overwhelming sadness and binge eating.

At first I felt a little odd to write a "good & bad" list on important people in my life. While doing my first T I was definitely taken over by very powerful emotions. Crying from such a deeper place than I ever have before, like a cleansing cry. The "finishing" emotions I felt while writing the letter brought it more together for me. I felt there were times with some the letter left me feeling complete for that T and other times brought me peace and happiness. The burning really brings it all together, rebirth of your soul through the fire. With every T that I have done I have walked away from the burning feeling lighter in my soul, having this sense/feeling of my beautiful soul glowing brighter.

I have been in "typical talk therapy" and it has never really done much for me. When I started receiving services from Amy I must admit I was cautiously optimistic, while also knowing she was the right person for me. Amy brings far more than "how did that make you feel?" or "describe the emotion you felt in that moment." She brings genuine care and wants to truly see you conquer each hill you have to climb. She will push you in all of the best ways to truly grow the way that you can!

Before Amy I really didn't see how much I didn't love myself and value myself. Working with her I can not only finally look myself in the eyes and say I Love You! But I also respect and value myself enough that I can finally make my dreams a priority. The confidence I now have for myself is indescribable. I am 38 years old and have never had the confidence that I feel inside of me now. She guided me down this path of glowing inside and shining bright!

I feel that T therapy is absolutely something that I can always get use out of. I feel there is still growing that I can do and I can see myself continue to utilize T therapy.

J. Rowe, Florida.

I came to Lady Bolding due to several issues I was having. I couldn't sleep without medication, my self-respect was at an all-time low, I couldn't celebrate my successes and my overall demeanor was horrible and I knew I needed to make a change if anything was going to change for me, so I reached out.

I thought T-Therapy was a waste of time and at first, I didn't take it too seriously. I felt stupid writing out what was in my head and quite frankly I was nervous about what would come out. However, I did the process as instructed, fought through the tough times of disbelief and fear as I uncovered certain things that I hadn't touched on before, but clearly were in my head. After the process, expecting immediate results, I was disappointed. It didn't take long for that disappointment to become one of those ahh-ha moments. I remember sitting back and thinking about something I was doing at the time, and I realized that I would have reacted a lot differently prior to my T-Therapy. It worked! I wasn't stressed. I wasn't weary of how it would turn out. I wasn't concerned at all and instinctively knew what I needed to do next. That was a glorious day!

The best part of Lady Bolding and what made her the perfect person to help me is the fact that everything she does, her motivation, experience, discipline and hard work, everything is derived from love. That's the foundation, everyone is wonderful and strong and capable and deserving, and her goal is to get everyone of us to see ourselves through her eyes. When we eventually do, we come out STRONG, DESERVING AND AMAZING. We become all of that and believe it, which makes the world a better place.

Since working with Lady Bolding, my life has changed 100%. Financially, I turned a corner and while working with her, increased my business revenue by 30%, putting me on track of smashing my goals. Emotionally, I am in tune with my inner Jim and understand what triggers the bad thoughts or what makes me smile, leaving me in complete control of my emotions and allowing me to grow with each new experience. Not to mention, I can use the T-Therapy whenever a situation comes up that requires that kind of attention. I NOW have the tools to combat what comes at me without allowing the baggage in. Oh, and for the first time in 10 years I can sleep without medication. I have not had a sleeping pill in over 15 months!

I am very happy to shout out for the whole world to hear that not only can I use T-Therapy for anything in the future, but that I ABSOLUTELY WILL. One T-Therapy session got rid of 40 years of baggage I had been carrying. This new tool I carry is a shining light leading me toward my future knowing that I got this. I'm going to check on Lady Bolding too, for refresher courses, maybe get her on the payroll somehow. She is the real deal!

J. Barron, California.

I was tired of wearing a mask and I wanted to be more open and vulnerable with my husband, but due to past traumas, I had a hard time being completely open and real and I felt like I was cheating. Because I felt like I wasn't loving him to the full potential that he deserved.

T therapy was a struggle in the beginning when it came to being real with how I felt and I blamed myself for all the things that happened to me in my past. I had to relive moments of my life that I never wanted to think or feel again, but because I did, I am now free. I have so much peace, love, and gratitude in my heart, mind, and soul. T therapy started to get easier and I learned that I was safe to say how I truly felt. There were even times where I had to do a few weeks on the same person because I wasn't being completely honest with myself. This usually happened when that individual had such a huge impact on my life and broke me the most. T therapy really helped me realize that all the things I thought about myself weren't true. That every feeling that I felt was real, because it happened. And just because it happened doesn't mean that it made me a bad person. T therapy lifted off decades of trauma and pain that I held on to because I was afraid if anyone knew about my past they would think of me as being tainted and dirty. It helped me realize that I was protecting the inner child of me that was left hurt and abandoned.

I would recommend Amy to everyone. Her voice is so warm, calm, and welcoming. She gives you a feeling of wanting to open up and you could without ever feeling an ounce of judgment. She makes you feel comfortable, loved, and most of all, IMPORTANT.

Working with Amy made me realize how much I deserve in life and how loved and important I am. I can now look in the mirror and say "I LOVE YOU " outloud without closing my eyes, turning my head, or crying uncontrollably. She took the mask that I have worn for decades and she shattered it. I have never been so happy as I am today. I still have moments of doubt, but I remember to use my ABC of gratitude and it makes the dark moments turn back to light.

THANK YOU Amy for believing in me, never giving up on me when I didn't believe in myself, or when I took 1 step forward to just fall 3 steps back. You have healed me in areas that I never thought were broken. You helped me find the life I have always urned for. You have boosted my confidence so much and taught me the true meaning and feeling to be LOVED. "LOVE ALWAYS WINS"!

T therapy is something that I will continue to use for the rest of my life. You will meet people in your life and not all are meant to stay forever. Doing T therapy on them will help you get through the heartache you may be feeling during the time of their departure from your life.

CONTENT

CHAPTER 1

SOMETHING HAS TO GIVE!

I'm trying, but nothing seems to work!

Sleepless nights, constant worry, feeling overwhelmed and defeated- do any of these sound familiar? I can relate. I felt like life was on an every 2 year repeat button. I'd gain traction and the shoe would drop. I would feel like things were ok, then I would see the same scenarios reappear in my life. It didn't matter where I'd move to, what job I'd get promoted to, how much money I made, what people would come in or out of my life. I would still end up with a mind full of worry and a heart feeling overwhelmed. I had tried the things "suggested" for my situation, such as positive affirmations, goal setting, podcasts, meditation, prayer, and of course I had to search google for answers to my issues.

I had considered some not so traditional methods as well such as, hypnotherapy, walking on fire, fasting, and even moving to a foreign country in pursuit of a complete reset. I tried recalling grandma's lectures, and big brother's advice. I even got on my knees and prayed for a wise husband to come into my life and give me guidance. I attended classes, courses, and masterclasses. I doubled up on prayer, meditation, walks, grounding, reading, and the list goes on! I tried many things. Though these things proved to work momentarily, it didn't create a lasting effect. The worry would resurface, the feeling of hopelessness, loneliness, and confusion would all slowly but surely return. It was hard to obtain quality sleep as my quiet time became a worry session.

So if this is you, hang in there, you got this, and things can get better. Which is why I have to share T therapy with the world! The techniques I mentioned above are all VALUABLE. There are many roads that may help you heal. I have done (and do) many of the aforementioned techniques, however before **ANY** of them had any lasting effect, or an ability to help me, there was something I had to do FIRST. Which is what this book is all about.

Telling myself I was all these wonderful things with I AM statements, while chanting positive affirmations had no lasting effect. Listening to other people tell me to believe in myself, or to master my thoughts helped me momentarily, and sounded right, but I just didn't find long term benefits from it. Being told to read the bible, or to pray longer, left me feeling wrong for what I was feeling, then guilt would set in. I had no doubt God loved me, but I will admit there was a slight disconnection in my love and understanding of him.

Practicing meditation in the midst of my storms, led me further down the road of frustration because I wondered -WHY IS THIS NOT WORKING FOR ME?!!! I had watched videos, read books, asked those who were practicing, why am I not getting anything from meditation and prayer? I had come to realize, there was an entire mountain I had to cross with **MYSELF** before ANY technique stood a chance in helping me long term. I was **blocked**. I was so full of self rationalizations from past experiences that it left no room for acceptance of anything else. And it certainly left no room to think forward. I had to find **ME**, and bring ME along in my life's journey- as weird as that may sound. I had to include ME. The first issue with this was, <u>I did not know ME</u>, and that there was more to me than this person I have seen in the mirror all these years. I was buried and didn't know it. I was in a deep, dark "valley" hosted by this thing called life. I was walking on pieces of my brokenness and learning how to avoid parts of myself. I had no clue how deep the hurt was, and how deep I had tried to bury it.

"The only true wisdom is in knowing you know nothing."
- Socrates

It was a Godsend

I was at a point of total surrender, my life didn't make sense anymore. I cried from the depths of my stomach through my heart, and out of the windows of my soul. With everything in me I looked up to the clouds and cried out, "God if you are really there, if you truly exist, and you are the loving God they say you are, and if we all have the same access to a great life, **WHY** am I here <u>digging in the dumpster at 40 years old!</u> **Why** have you let this happen? I am a good person! Was my childhood not torture enough? I am challenging **everything** I have heard and was told to believe about you, I WANT a loving, beautiful, and abundant life! Prove to me your love is real, let me know I am not alone. If not, I don't know if I can go on. I am tired. God, I am **claiming** every single promise in the bible!"

Cold tears of exhaustion, pain, frustration, and confusion ran down my face and I watched my entire life play back in my mind like a movie. I had never felt such pain or despair. I felt pain for who I was, for what I had been through, and couldn't help but wonder- isn't enough, enough? For the first time in my life I felt **hopeless,** and completely <u>alone.</u>

I wish I could tell you that after all that screaming and crying, the flood gates of heaven opened up and all my problems were solved. **Nope**, not so much. It was the opposite, **I was called to work.** Deep, life changing work. Without going too far into the story, (there is another book for that), when T therapy came about I was at the end of my rope. An unfortunate circumstance had led me to some of the darkest moments in my adult life. Which had me in the dumpster looking for recycling to survive. There were times as I was digging in that trash can I wondered, how these hands that were once allowed to give cpr to a flatlined person, are now digging in dumpsters for survival.

Life can often take sick **twists** and turns, that may leave you looking in the mirror staring at what feels like a total stranger. When it does, it can create a feeling of loss and confusion. This is usually when finding something to help **cope** comes into play. For some- it's drugs, alcohol, sex, over working, over eating, sleep aids, prescription pills, a cycle of toxic relationships, self destructive behaviors- cutting, anorexia, bulimia. Or maybe an overwhelming amount of egotism, self righteousness, title affixation, or complete denial, you name it, it's out there.

This book is not just a book of feelings and experiences, it is a **toolbox**. You will learn **techniques** with a primary focus on T therapy.

T Therapy has been successful around the globe. You will become more aware, more full and vibrant, leading you to living a more loving and peaceful life.

Results may vary, but this method is proven to work. The difference in the results depends on <u>how much of yourself you allow to be present in the work</u>. I am thankful for the opportunity to share this technique with you. The journey will be filled with **highs and lows**, but the benefits are freeing, rewarding, and unforgettable. Learning this technique is something you can use forever. Trust me when I say, you will never want to go back to the old way of thinking and feeling. Your life is such a gift, and once you decide to take yourself seriously, and do the work mentioned in between these pages, your life can be changed forever. The choice is yours!

"If you want something you've never had, you must be willing to do something you've never done." - *Thomas Jefferson*

Choosing this book and taking it to the checkout counter is the first step. **<u>Do not proceed until you are ready.</u>** Readiness is key. Are you ready to take **YOU** seriously and to become aware of your best self? Love is **ALWAYS** the answer, and if you are ready to return to love, and drop the heaviness, let's get started. You're worth it!

CHAPTER 2

THE JOURNEY

Here comes T Therapy

Then came along T therapy. In doing the work of T Therapy, I had to face my shadows, eradicate distortions in my thinking, and address things I had thrown under the rug. I needed to rid my past in a **healthy**, and **systematic** way while **healing** at the same time. That in itself is a tall order. Being in the medical field for over 10 years and studying human behavior, I was aware there is a mind and body relationship that creates a response systemically. I understood the power of the subconscious mind, the programming, the importance of emotions and the environment as early on as embryonic development, and the effects it has on the child even before birth and throughout childhood. These years are so often overlooked as potential resources for understanding current emotional patterns and behavior. For the most part childhood is remembered for many good things thankfully and not the ugly dysfunction that many of us survived in that we had viewed as normal. Then one day it all catches up to us. Sure I had all this information, I had studied it, <u>but I didn't see how it shows up in what looks like a healthy functioning adult.</u> Particularly me.

I felt I had done well holding onto life, making changes as they were required, accepting highs and lows of life. Then I realized my changes were

reactions, instead of <u>solutions</u>. So if you are wondering why you are not getting lasting results when you are "**changing**" yourself, I would say- you may not need to "change" yourself as much as you may need to <u>**"heal"**</u> and understand yourself. You have to genuinely <u>**allow**</u> for healing to happen.

Over time we build walls that we forgot we put there, we allow excuses, protect our wounds, and we start to avoid things. We become better liars as adults than we were as children avoiding punishment. The worst part, the majority of the lying is lying to ourselves. Pretending everything is ok. Then that becomes our truth, and the basis of who we are. It's one of the unfortunate ways adults cope at times, we just avoid, dismiss, ignore, blame, or excuse it. <u>**We just don't want to deal with it!**</u> To put it straight forward, we become very hard headed as adults, and we <u>don't like to do what we don't want to do.</u> Even if it is beneficial to us, many times we don't like to be uncomfortable, nor do we want to do the **necessary work**. We try to find a shortcut in doing the work, or pay someone else to do it. That may work for some things but not for all things.

> **"Be brave enough to heal yourself even when it hurts."**
> *- Bianca Sparacino*

Layers

We are people of many layers. We tend to bury some things deeper than others. For most adults we like to believe **"I'll forget it, and it will go away."** or, we like to be the tough one and say things like, "why cry over spilled milk, the past is the past."

We go on as if the traumas, dysfunctions, or painful things that happened to us in our childhood, youth, or even adulthood just fade away all on their own.

I think it is pretty **amazing** how we are able to just "**go on**" after many painful life experiences that had the potential to destroy us. Unfortunately, it eventually **catches up** with us. I have clients as young as 21 and as seasoned as 72. **<u>You don't outrun life</u>**, it is with you the whole time waiting for you to face it. When the time comes to face yourself, it doesn't usually come with a dozen roses and a sweet note card saying, "deal with your inner self please." It usually comes with a little more urgency. Many times the message for change comes in harsh reality checks. They sound a little like this:

"Start taking this high blood pressure medication"

"You are now borderline diabetic."

"I am sorry, I am leaving, it's over."

"Why are you always so angry?"

The truth is, disease is simply just that, a form of **DIS-EASE.** What shows up on the outside is simply a reflection of what is going on inside. It's been proven time and time again that we **ARE** a product of our environment. I am not referring only to geographical references but mental, emotional, and physical environments as well. **We can only be- who we are.** That may take saying a few times before it is fully understood, and for me, it took over 40 years to get it. So I say it again, we can only be **WHO WE ARE.**

<u>Who we are comes from a place deeper than the eye can see</u>, it's not what they call us, it's not who they pay us to be. It's not who they expect us to be. It's not who we aspire to be. Who we have become is the total sum of our experiences, and who we feel we need to be because of them. Then we play out our current realities based on those experiences. That makes us who we have become. This however doesn't mean this is who we truly are. Have you ever asked someone why they do something and they tell you their dad did it that way? Or you ask someone why they don't try something and they tell you it's because they tried it 15 years ago? Or you ask someone if they

like onions, they say no and when you ask them why they don't', and they say, I don't know, I just don't like the way they smell. Letting experiences shape our realities can cause serious hindrances in our growth. Some experiences shape us in a good way, but some not so good. Either way, we change because of our life experiences whether we are aware of it or not.

If we have a part of our past that is rotten and spoils our present moments, keeping us from our total self, we are **not** who we think we are, we are simply surviving and avoiding, which keeps us from our **truest self**. (You may want to reread that sentence, it said a lot). Avoiding healing, or **ignoring** the need to heal will leave you feeling **trapped, suffocated, limited**, and **fearful**. Fear will keep you looking for constant distractions, and knee deep in constant avoidance. You may feel like nothing in the world bothers you "<u>most of the time</u>" **until** you're alone with yourself. Or the times something in life "pokes the bear" as I like to call it, then you **spiral** into an unavoidable, unexplainable **ugly** part of yourself. That place is usually dark, sad, leaving you feeling alone, and misunderstood. Then you start thinking of ways get **far away** from what you are feeling.

As mentioned in the intro of this book, as people we tend to find a way of removing ourselves from moments of unwanted feelings by finding a distraction or a vice. Unfortunately what you will find is- no matter **how deep you have buried things**, either intentionally, or even unintentionally, you <u>will</u> continue to run from your shadows until you decide to **face them**.

"You can't get away from yourself by moving from one place to another." - *Earnest Hemingway*

Why Now?

It happens for people at different times in their life. I have clients that didn't start looking deeper into themselves until they were in their 70's. It is **never too late** to do this work, and it is **never too early** to start this work.

It is important to know that healing is NOT linear. It is more like a puzzle at times. One day you find all the fitting pieces then the next day nothing seems to fit right. However, everything you need is in that box, one piece at a time. The same is true with healing. Some stages are frustrating and it seems everything you try doesn't fit, but the truth is, everything you need is within you, it just requires you to work on it. The healed you is within you, you just have to be present and willing to put it together.

It delights me to see the younger generation taking time to find their true selves. I have heard many call the younger generation lazy. I won't get into that debate, but I will say this: <u>The younger generation is realizing how important it is to understand oneself</u>, and make what's in their best interest a priority.

They are finding ways to be creative, and to do things smarter, and not harder. They've learned how to use technology to do heavy lifting, and create a great income from it. So I will say this, may their journey to their best self (which only helps us all in the long run) continue to forge forward, and may they pick up a rake or tool and do a little labor along the way. A little yard work never hurts anybody!

New experiences call for a new way of thinking, remember that sentence as I introduce you to T therapy. Let me repeat it for you- <u>New experiences, call for new ways of thinking</u>. Anytime you hesitate in making positive changes in your life, and start to quit on yourself, remember that sentence. If you want to produce, experience, and become your best self, you have to do some things that may seem <u>unfamiliar</u>, less traditional, and quite frankly unheard of at times. <u>If you don't try to do life differently than you have been doing all these years, then you already know your future.</u> Just take today and fast forward 20 years. If you don't change mentally and emotionally there will be no change. You will just get older. Your physical features may change, but your mental health won't. At least not in a positive way. I am sure you can look into your life right now and think of someone who is <u>still</u> doing the **same** things, <u>talking</u> about the **same** things, and <u>dealing</u> with things the same way as they were in high school. Yet, they wonder why life is treating them the same way. They have not moved forward, they are stuck on the repeat button.

If you want the **most** of yourself and your life, you have to look into your present moment, and say, I'm **ready** to grow. Today is a new day, and a **new** me. I am **ready** for a shift. I am ready to peel back the layers, and get to my best self. **I am ready to do the work**. Do you want to feel **peace**? Do you want to be mentally and emotionally **free**? You have to accept where you are right now, and be **ready** to go <u>forward</u>, to be vulnerable, open, and to make the decision to do the work.

"Don't contaminate your future with the
backwash of your past." *-Lady B.*

CHAPTER 3

GOING IN!

It's not a quick fix!

I will get a call every now and then from a potential client, and they are like a **hot potato**, something has ticked them off and they want help **NOW**!! I mean they want to start today! In that very minute, they are "ready!". The sad part, generally these individuals never become clients because they want the "fix it now" answers to their current situation, and are not wanting to do <u>the work</u>. Sad but true.

There was a lady who had been beaten by her spouse for many years, and wanted to leave, she messaged and asked to become one of my clients. I asked her a few questions about why she feels she is ready for help and after a short conversation, she <u>decided she really didn't want help or change</u>. Later to find out she **continued to find abuse** in her life to feed her **need** of acceptance which to her was felt, and assured by abuse. She had so much of her life infused with abuse, it felt like home. The thought of leaving that situation, and trusting a life she never knew seemed too great of a risk for her. She had created what we call a comfort zone. Don't be fooled, not all comfort is good or healthy. It simply means, I have come to know this situation, I will stay in this situation because I feel it is safer than the unknown.

I pray for her, and those in that situation. Believing that they will find the courage to walk away and heal. Walking away is usually temporary if you don't heal. This is why for many in this situation they see repeated toxic partnerships/relationships/situationships in their life. **What isn't healed and completed, will be repeated.** Write that down, you may need to refer to that one day.

For some it is **easy to see** the "abuse" as it is happening to them, for others it's more of a **silent** and slow turning self destructive process. There are people who are victims of what looks like a more socially acceptable form of self destruction such as over working, self isolation, self hatred, self medicating, legal drug addiction, all just to avoid their life. Many may wonder why a person stays with an abusive partner, because they see it as a stupid thing to do, and look at the victim as one who doesn't love themself, but yet those same assumptions are never thought about man or woman that overeats to run from their feelings. Abuse is abuse even when you are the one doing it to yourself. It just seems unjust when another is doing it to us. Sometimes we are the WORST at mentally abusing ourselves, we don't need anyone's help. That was a bit of harsh truth, but we teach people how to treat us, and it starts with the way we treat ourselves.

We are all the same, but different. Let that be the first thing to be understood. Audrey Hepburn said it best when she said, "**Nothing is more important than empathy for another human being's suffering. Not a career, not wealth, not intelligence. Certainly not status. We have to feel for one another if we're going to survive with dignity.**"

I'll add, you cannot know empathy for another if you first don't know it for yourself. Now, right now. Now is the best time to start the change. Please don't feel that it's too late, or that you are not worthy of a great life. Please don't feel you are only born to work, pay bills, and die. Ouch! You are worth it! Now let's start talking about T therapy. **I am proud of you**, self work is the hardest, yet most <u>rewarding</u> work you'll <u>ever</u> journey into, **you got this!**

"You are always one choice away from changing your life."
- Mac Anderson

Do I have to do this alone?

In short, yes. In truth, you're never really alone. A part of the reason I feel this technique has proven to be so effective is because it is **personal work** that should be done in private. I do want to make it clear -that it is best if you do have an **emotional accountability partner** (a coach, spouse, family member, therapist, someone who can be a healthy and positive support system) while going through this. Here is something I want you to get from this journey that you are about to embark on, there is not one single person who can do the work of self, other than **self**. Yes, this means you. It is a solo walk into yourself that takes <u>every ounce of you</u> to participate in order to be **effective**. This is why a lot of people would rather not do it. It is easier for some to just live the life of a robot doing the same things day in and day out, and when bad feelings come up, they'd rather just numb it. No matter how much your family, spouse, children, relatives, friends love you, <u>they</u> **<u>cannot</u>** <u>do this part for you</u>. Sure you can call them and talk about what is bothering you, and get perspective on things but they can't go INSIDE **you** and do the internal work that needs to be done. <u>They are giving you feedback based on what is inside of them.</u>

Let me start by asking you this, who is reading this book right now? And here is your answer- YOU. I believe in you, please know you will be better for doing this work. You will go through the work alone but at the same time, you also are the one who gets the freedom that comes from doing it.

While you are doing your T's, make it a time when you will not be interrupted or distracted. The setting in which you do it should be in a place that makes you **feel** safe, so you can be <u>open and transparent</u>. Sometimes when we feel we have to tend to people or things around us we get distracted. The work of the T will require your full attention for best results. So give this work your all.

This process calls for vulnerability and self trust. If you have a partner who is loving enough to just "be there" to hold you after completing your T's, you are in good shape. However this won't be the case for everyone. For some- you will be doing it by yourself from start to finish. I will never forget a client telling me about her spouse and how he would wait by the door for the burning process of the T to finish and just be there for her when she walked through the door to hold her. Not to ask her questions, but simply to hold her. That is so powerful!

Group T Therapy: Group T Therapy is very effective with a trained guide. I advise anyone who has intentions on leading a group to contact me, or take a course first to understand the complexities of group T therapy. These are very good for youth groups, men and women groups, rehab groups, self help groups, and more. There is something to be honored and valued about collective energy. When you provide a safe place for those seeking healing, this is truly a gift.

> **"If you change the way you look at things, the things you look at change."** - *Wayne Dyer*

How long will the process take?

Please read this section carefully. This process can take months. Each T however only takes a few days at a time. If you feel like that is a long time, I want you to look in the mirror and ask yourself how long you've been carrying unnecessary emotional trauma and baggage around. I believe for most, it has been way more than a few months. For me, it was 40 years. Please don't be discouraged. Know that once you become comfortable with the process, you start to look forward to doing T's. It becomes a tool you really enjoy having around. If done correctly, T therapy can change your life.

Now, here is a very important part to remember- THIS PROCESS IS TIME SENSITIVE. When starting these T's, **do not leave them open for more than 2 days.** Be sure when you are starting one, you are in a position to finish it within 2 days. The reason for this is- **energy**. I use this example with my clients: it's like leaving the front door open on the coldest winter day of the year, the draft comes in your warm house and eventually takes it over. Shut the front door to that cold asap, but with good diligence. **Do not rush the process, and at the same time do not drag your feet about it either.** Once you start the process, <u>you need to finish it.</u> I will explain the steps in greater detail in the getting started portion of this book.

The other rule for time with this work is, easy does it. **Do not get ahead of the emotional processing**. <u>There is no getting them all done back to back</u>. There is **no** rushing to get it done. Scratching the surface to just get the work done is **harmful**, and a **waste of time** because it will need to be re done. <u>Give yourself at least a week in between T's.</u> **This is very important**. You need time for **emotional processing**. You will feel a change, a lightness, a freedom, and a positive awareness in your emotional energy after each T. Within the week you may feel a sense of loss, this is normal. Loss just means something isn't there anymore. It will go away. You will fill that space with something beautiful in time. You may also feel a little emotional in the week following the completion of a T. This too is normal, this is a calibration period. You'll be fine. Allow your emotions to be what they are, let them come and watch them go. **<u>This is a time when you honor your emotions, feel it, and allow yourself to be free of it.</u>**

In time, you will feel that lightness and freedom feeling I mentioned. For some it's as soon as they burn it, for others it happens two or three days later.

Everyone will process differently. This is why you need a week or even two inbetween T's, and again, you should never RUSH to get it done. This is not a school, work, or a honey do list assignment. This is life work, it is serious business. It is to be **respected**, and the process is to be **honored**. <u>Please re read this section as needed.</u>

"Healing doesn't mean the damage never existed. It means it no longer controls our life" - *Ashkay Dubeyy*

"The poison leaves bit by bit, not all at once. Be patient. You are healing"- *Yasmin Mogahed*

CHAPTER 4

EXPECTATIONS

What should I expect during and after this process?

Freedom, peace, relief, openness, tranquility, joy, clarity, and happiness, and even healthy amnesia. Many forget all about the anger or sadness they felt about this person or situation they had once felt prior to doing the T. This is a good thing, it means you **properly did your T's,** and you are healing.

I will always remember the day I started my processes with T therapy. I was guided every step of the way. **I truly thought I had lost my mind**. Why was I doing this? Why was I going down memory lane, a place of such dark, shattered, and painful moments? I was sitting in the kitchen at a small table next to the window in an oversized blue robe, a pair of french connection sunglasses, a pen and a notebook. My son walked past me as he was headed to work, and asked, "Are you ok mom?" I said yes, and he asked why I had sunglasses on inside the house. I told him it helps me to concentrate. No judging, it wasn't a lie.

The truth was, it made me feel invisible. <u>I was preparing to meet the pains that rested deep down in my soul- and being comfortable was important.</u>

So for this mission I had hot yogi tea, an oversized blue fluffy robe, and a pair of shades. I was waiting for him to leave so I could begin another day of T therapy. **<u>I want to stress again the importance of feeling safe enough to be vulnerable.</u>** This will require true focus and intention. Something wonderful happens with every part of this process. Words cannot describe the emotional shifts you will feel with each step. You will feel a wide spectrum of emotions, and you should. You will feel sad, mad, disappointed, and even pain, to name a few. I cried so much I couldn't breathe through my nose, and I hadn't done that since I was a kid! You may feel like this through some of the process, then in the next step you feel so free that you cry tears of joy.

There are 5 steps to this process. **All steps** serve a very important purpose. Do not skip, rush, or avoid anything you feel. It will pay off in the end. I have clients who tried to tell me they did a T on someone and by their energy alone, I knew they didn't. **This process is transformational**. You will tell the difference in your life during and after doing a T. <u>So expect to experience a version of yourself you had never had the opportunity to experience.</u>

I think it is pretty amazing how we have an ability to continue to achieve and pursue things in life even with the weight of our past quietly pulling us down. It's **unfortunate** how much **time we have lost**, how many experiences we have **mistreated**, and how many endeavors we have missed out on for the sake of old baggage we were bound by. Here is the silver lining in that- how amazing is it that you stayed strong, and figured out how to survive in the midst of your chaos? You are pretty awesome to have pulled that off! Now think about how wonderful life will be **once you lay all of those burdens down, and begin to live with peace.** It is truly a gift, it is living.

"Healing is the end of conflict within yourself"
- Stephanie Gailing

**"Come to me, all you who are weary and burdened,
and I will give you rest"** *- Matthew 11:28*

What happens once all my T's are done?

It's never truly done. It's a gift that keeps on giving! This is a process, and you will find that over time a person or experience may come up, and you will be happy and prepared to eagerly do a T.

What you do <u>after</u> the T's are done is **very important**. It is like having the most vulnerable, new, and healthy soil in the world at your fingertips ready to grow anything you like. You are <u>new</u>, fresh, open, healthy ground. It is time to start planting <u>new</u> things where the pain once was. <u>New</u> experiences, beliefs, habits, norms, friends, hobbies, and the list goes on. You may even feel the desire to do something you always wanted to, such as play an instrument, sky dive, paint, sing, go back to school, or build something. It is an amazing **transformation**.

Once I had completed my T's, I started meditating, praying differently, reading more, writing, creating, traveling, and doing new things. I truly felt wonderful. I started living with a deeper faith, falling deeper and deeper in love with myself, and I became conscious of mind, body, and soul. I began trusting myself in a way I had never done before. **I leaned IN on life for the first time.** Instead of leaning back and resisting or avoiding it.

I went from wondering what others think of me, to not even noticing the people around me. I became one with each and every moment of my days. I was no longer separated by thoughts, but living in my moments.

What you need to catch here is, I was at the lowest point of my adult life, I was on the brink of suicide, I was going to bed hungry, I was being rejected by job after job, I was living in an area where homicide teams were seen on a regular. It was like I was in a time warp shipped back to my childhood, and even in that grave of a condition, even <u>before anything changed externally</u> or in my environment, I felt a change <u>within</u>. **ONCE I CHANGED THE INSIDE,** the outside followed suit. So I say this with great sincerity, **please don't wait** <u>for the ocean or storm of your life to be calm to start making changes within, choose to do it even in the midst of the storm</u>! This is a process like no other. **It will change your life.** You are one decision away from a new chapter in <u>your</u> book of life.

Let's get to it!

<u>READ THE ENTIRE BOOK BEFORE YOU START.</u>

Before I guide you step by step I want to give you a few rules. Yes rules, disclaimers, etc. For starters, this therapy will change your life <u>**if**</u> you do it <u>fully and wholeheartedly.</u> **It is a deep work**, and will bring forth powerful emotions. I advise you to do this exercise **totally free of any substance**. It is not a time to be in an altered emotional state, it is a time to be present. If that is not something you can do, you may want to consider a different technique. If you feel you are not in a good emotional state to handle this, please do it **when you feel you can**. I have advised all my clients, from not just an awareness coach perspective but from me being a nurse as well, to take a daily multivitamin, b12, and vitamin C if you are up for it. Anytime we add stressors to our body it is important to support ourselves anyway we can. Drink adequate amounts of water, staying hydrated plays a big role in a healthy mind and body as well as cellular repair. Please know you don't have to, I just found it helps. I am not prescribing here, just advocating for balance.

If you are in a relationship, married, etc, please know your partner may feel a bit **excluded** during some of this process. Men feel the need to protect and want to fight our battles for us, and women have a tendency to want to nurture. **Love is who we are at the core**, so understanding what our loved one is going through helps us to feel more comfortable not being able to help the way we are used to. I have found the best way to avoid making them feel some type of way is to **let them in** on the fact you are about to do some **deep diving emotional work**, so if you are out of your normal sorts, it is to be expected.

<u>Do not be ashamed of working on yourself.</u> I just know a partner can feel shut out if they are not aware of their significant other going through this process. I will also add, if you are in a toxic relationship, healing is hard to do. As it has been said, you can't expect to heal being in the same environment that makes you sick. I would also advise that you keep this process to yourself until it is completed. Sometimes the opinions of others can taint your canvas. You do not need a person's opinion or approval to work on yourself. People will see the difference in you, and when they do, smile and tell them thank you.

As you write these T's work on them ONE AT A TIME. Giving yourself a week or longer in between each one. You will know when you are ready to move to the next one. **Do not start a T and leave it open.** What I mean by "leave it open" is- starting it without taking it to completion. Give yourself 2 days max to complete each T, with the exception of one which I will go over. Make the time and space dedicated solely for this work and not during a time when you're trying to multitask.

One of the most **important** disclaimers I want to mention is that there is a step of the T that requires burning, and as we know, fire can burn down a city, so please, on the step "burn your T" - **do so responsibly.** <u>When in doubt go the safe route, over a toilet, in a fireplace already lit, the kitchen</u>

sink, etc. Please be safe. **IF** you are a minor reading this please get adult supervision for this part. Another reminder is to be **comfortable** when doing this process. As I mentioned earlier, I was in an oversized robe, and sunglasses, by a window in broad daylight. I do suggest doing this when you are awake and alert. Sometimes starting this process before going to bed can cause you to have a rough night's sleep, remember, finishing the T is key.

Don't look for instant results (although very common), just allow yourself to feel, as it comes. Don't sit around waiting to feel something, once it is burned, it's done. You'll feel the results all on their own. You will notice the change. God Bless you, I believe in you. Leave your ego at the door, embrace yourself! I will see you on the other side. I am proud of you for taking on such a big task. I promise you it will be **WORTH IT!!**

> **"The only way to make sense out of change is to plunge into it, move with it, and join the dance."** -*Alan Watts*

CHAPTER 5
TEA TIME!

Step 1: The List

<u>**READ THE ENTIRE BOOK AND DIRECTIONS BEFORE YOU START**</u>

<u>**Make a list**</u> of anyone who has had an emotional anchor on your life. Good or bad. Think about your life starting with your childhood, and continue on until the present moment. I will help you with this list. Keep in mind, these can be people who were not or have not been active in your life, but actively stayed in your emotions. Such as absent parents, lost family members, even family members who passed away without you meeting them. If you were a foster kid, or adopted, do a T on the biological side that you never met. See the examples of people you may have on your list below:

Parents- if they were or weren't in your life, they are a must.

Siblings- you'd be surprised what comes out of you on this one.

Family members- if they pull at you emotionally, a T needs to be done.

Friendships- I have found even in my own life, I have had some friendships end that I never imagined would end. The unfortunate part, sometimes you don't always get to say much before it's gone. Thank goodness for the T.

Past relationships/marriages- as for the relationships, any long standing relationship, and ALL or ANY Marriages.

Teachers/Coaches/Bosses- I have found some of the worst mental hang ups we have come not just from family or the ones we love, but the ones we look up to. These experiences sting, and words stick, sometimes for a lifetime.

Any deep circumstances or experiences- girls homes, boys homes, jail, drug or alcohol addictions, abortions, personal regrets. Some things we need to rid ourselves of are not always people, <u>as much as they are experiences</u>. So if there was a situation where it wasn't a person but maybe some events in your life that need to be let go of, the T is what needs to be done.

Last but not least, the hardest one of them all, YOU. <u>Yes a T on you.</u>

Once you have made a well thought out and comprehensive list, it's time to go to step 2. You should see my clients face when they think they are all done all to find out they have one to do on themself! They do love me for it after, but nobody has been thrilled with the idea at first.

You can add to the list as you go, but <u>please don't short change this process</u>, just to get started. Creating this list is to be taken seriously. Give yourself a couple of days to add to it. Think of this list as designing the house of your dreams. With each section of this process you are building it piece by piece. How big do you want your home, and what type of view do you want? Take your time. Do it thoroughly.

Step 2: The T.

The suggested order to go in is Parents, siblings, family members, coaches/Teachers/Pastors/Leaders, Relationship/Marriage(s), Children, and last but not least, Self. You may not have people in each of these categories, but **do not avoid any** if you do. Please don't avoid, just embrace. Just to reiterate, if you had an absent parent or you were adopted or fostered, you still need to do a T on your parents both biological and adopted/foster. Just because someone was not present, does not mean you didn't have feelings about it. Do the work, it will pay off.

You will only do <u>**one T at a time**</u>. This is important. Making a T is just how it sounds, take a fresh sheet of paper, letter size, and make a big T in the middle of the page.

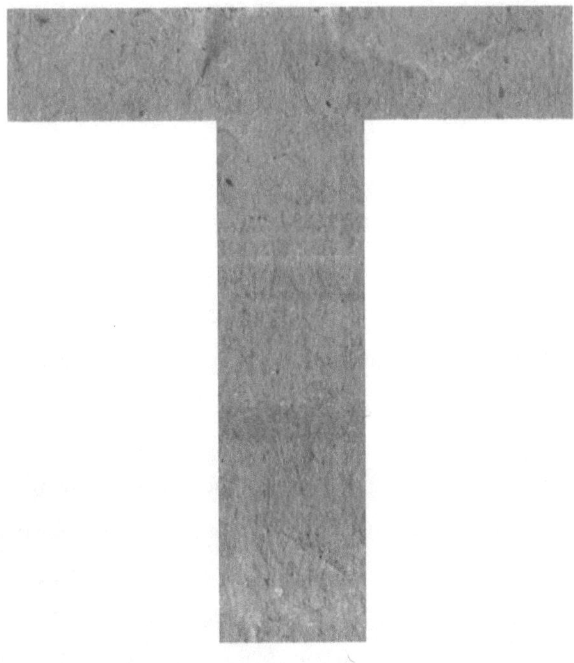

On the <u>top of your T write the name of the person you are doing the T on.</u> Write it big. <u>On the left side</u> of the T write down all the crappy things about your experience with this person. The things that hurt, the things you felt were unfulfilled, or painful, or wrong.

The KEY to this is to walk down memory lane, go there, go into the moment, bring up the emotion. Remember you are not doing this to hurt, you are doing this to properly address and <u>heal</u> so you can be done with it. You have to be petty, I want <u>every detail</u>. You cannot feel guilt for what you feel.

<u>You cannot reason as you are now, you have to accept how you felt then.</u> For instance if something happened at 8 that hurt your feelings, you can't look at it being 45 years (whatever your current age is) old find an excuse as to why it doesn't hurt now. We are dealing with the hurt that happened at 8, not the hurt you think you do or don't feel at your present age. **It is not your job to "understand" why someone did something to you.** Nor should you allow for excuses for their behavior. No more throwing things under the rug. This is the time to <u>honor the person you were at the time who went through it.</u>

I am going to help guide you through some of the things I feel are important to be brought up, because many times we feel "wrong" for feeling a certain way about our parents and family. We think it would make us seem ungrateful, or that we are fault finding. **<u>That is not the idea behind the work.</u>**

<u>On the right side of the T,</u> you will write the more favorable memories of the person or situation. This side can be hard to do for someone who has caused you pain. Below I have listed some of the items I listed on my own T's to help give you an example of how it is done. Some of these may be hard for you to read, but I want you to see the depth this activity calls for. I

will tell you ahead of time, not all these T's are going to be easy to read, feel free to skip them but please don't skip the instructions.

Scenario 1: A parent (My moms name was on the top of my T)

Right side: (This is the side of favorable things)

I loved the way you smiled at me and how your eyes would sparkle.

You were so beautiful. I felt special to be yours.

I loved the way you'd let me stand on the stool at the stove and help flip tortillas.

I loved the way you always took me places with you, even if they weren't the best places. You never wanted to leave me behind.

I loved the sound of your laugh.

I loved the time we went to the zoo.

I loved when you were home.

I loved when you were happy.

-      You catch the idea, these are a few of the things on my list.

Left side: (The less favored, hurtful side)

Why did you have to do drugs? I hated seeing you angry

I hated seeing you fight.

I hated seeing you drunk.

It hurt me to see you leave because I didn't know when you were coming back.

It hurt me to see you cry.

Why did you have to die, I wish you didn't leave me here alone.

I feel like if you would have just tried harder to be better you would have lived longer.

When you died my life was horrible. Bad things have happened to me for many years.

I hate that I can't remember your voice, I just remember you coming and going.

- You get the idea, these are just a few of the things I wrote.

Scenario 2: An Abuser

There will be some T's you will do that may be on someone who has physically assaulted, or harmed you. These **are not easy** to do, but **necessary**. I want you to be open, vulnerable, and allow for emotions. I want you to go back into the feelings of whenever, wherever, however it happened, and **feel** what was there, at that time of the incident. **You are safe. You are loved. You can do this**. Please remember we are not seeking to keep the pain, we are going to restore, release, forgive, and be free from this. As I have mentioned before, when doing these T's please be comfortable, in a warm blanket, a robe, and in a place that makes you feel safe to be open and vulnerable. You got this! *You're worth it!* Below I have given you parts of the T from one of my abusers so you can see some of the things that may come up for you, and how you need to be detailed. The **more detailed** you are the less you leave behind to ruminate. Just think of it as you sweeping off the porch, why sweep half of it, sweep the whole thing. Same with this, get it all out.

My abuser (You want to put a name here, not "my abuser" if you know their name)

Right side:
I thought you were cool when I was younger.
We loved the same kind of chocolate.
You are a child of God too.

(Remember, this side of the list may be very short, especially for someone who has assaulted you. Sometimes all I had for this side is, you are human, or you

are God's child too. And that's ok! But love is always the answer, so if we can just try to find something, it is beneficial.)

Left side:

I hated how you made me sit on your lap so you could touch me.

I hated the heat off your breath when you would breathe on me.

I hated how you made me feel so scared.

I hated the way it felt when you would force yourself on me.

I hated how you acted like you never did this to me.

I hate that you never apologized or asked for forgiveness when I got older.

I hate that a family member could do this. You are supposed to be able to trust your family.

I hate that you made me hate intercourse as an adult because of what you did.

I hate that as an adult I hated my body because you used it and abused it.

(You get the point) I was trying to not be too explicit with the abuse, but you see how I had to use specific details. As you pour onto the Left side of that T you should feel things get lighter. This is only step 2, step 3 will also bring more freedom, then step 4, will bring more, then step 5. Be present in EVERY SINGLE step. Each step is important.

I am going to give you a few more scenarios based on my own life. Hopefully this will help you if you should get stuck or hit a brick wall with your feelings, which is a common thing. In the years of ignoring our pain we build blinders and create a level of amnesia. It is all a protective mechanism. Many times we have become so good at burying our feelings it takes work to bring them back into the light, give yourself time.

Scenario 3:Relationship(s)

Relationships/Marriages are such **monumental influences** in our life. This T is so important because without letting it go, you will continue to waste time continually using that pain as a reference point. You will be looking through eyes of regret, versus eyes of optimism. You will seek partnerships that prove the other ones wrong, instead of allowing the right connections to just happen. <u>**You can't receive with a clenched fist and a closed heart!**</u> So, let the work begin. You got this! You're worth it!

<u>Relationship</u> (again you will put a name at the top of the T)

Right side:
I loved the way you adored your kids.
I loved your smile.
I loved holding your hand.
I loved when you sent my flowers, you really knew how to pick them.
I loved our pictures, we were cute together.
I loved when you sent random "thinking of you/love you texts."

Left side:
I didn't like when you were angry.
I didn't like who you became when you drank.
I hated when you would flirt with women in front of me.
I hated that you cheated.
I was afraid when you would yell and threaten.
I was afraid when you would speed when I was in the car to try and scare me.
You never held me.
You never asked me how my projects were going, you didn't care about who I was as a person.
We never had conversations about goals.

You rarely said thank you.

- You get the idea, these are just a few of the things on my list. Sometimes your list will be so long, you don't think you will ever stop writing! Don't feel guilty, don't judge it, just LET IT OUT! That is what this is about. You will find more will come out in the next step as well.

Again, you must be **honest, open, and even petty** in this step. You are not trying to PROVE yourself or them WRONG OR RIGHT. You are simply being 100% transparent with what <u>YOU</u> feel. There is no wrong word or statement here, this is all about you and you.

One of the most powerful T's you will do is on **yourself**. This is the final T, for the scheduled T's anyway. The order to this is important. Doing yourself first with a T would be a **very unfair quest**, as you have to peel back some of what made you- you before you just start listing the likes and dislikes of yourself. By doing the other T's first, you give yourself a true chance of reflecting on yourself openly and honestly without some of the hang ups, hurts, barriers, undue inflictions, and partiality.

Take your time with this T, as you should with any of them. Remember, you do not want to leave a T started and unfinished, "open" as I call it. It's like leaving the front door in a warm house open on a cold winter day, but for this T, take your time. If you need a week to do this one, be kind, give yourself a week. Just know you may feel a slight roller coaster of emotions. <u>You may also find that everything in the world gets in your way of completing this particular T.</u> Not to spoil the fun, but it's because you have become professional at making **everything else** important but yourself. Time to change that. I don't advise taking longer than a week to finish. You should be looking at it and working on it daily. Even if that means staring at it, and nothing comes out, it will eventually start to flow. I will give you a glimpse into my T on self, so you can get an idea.

Scenario 4: Self T

AMY (your name should be at the top of the T)

Right Side:

You survived- a childhood of abuse, abandonment, loneliness, and being parentless. You survived physical abuse from relationships.

You still have an open heart even after all you went through. You never went for revenge, you just let things go.

You continuously seek knowledge and ways to grow.

You are so loving.

You hold yourself accountable even when you don't like it.

You always see the bright side of things.

You follow your heart.

You believe the best in and for people even if they can't see it for or in themselves.

You give in so many ways.

You always see the possible even in the most impossible situations.

You are always open to the different seasons of life.

The way you never gave up on yourself.

You chose to forgive those that most would have never forgiven.

(These are some I listed, just to give you some insight, try to use specific examples)

The Left Side: (This side may hurt to write, but it needs to all come out. Be honest, and let it go. Details are important)

You want love and sometimes you spend too long in relationships that no longer serve you. You fix what's not for you to fix.

My body is not where I want it to be, and sometimes I feel ashamed of it. I get upset with myself because I don't stay committed to a workout routine.

I committed recklessly in my past, and should have healed so I could have chosen healthier relationships.

I wish I would have coddled my sons more when they were younger. I was too busy working. I wish I would have taken more time with them.

I don't like that you blame yourself for being a single parent.

I spent many years in anger, which was such a waste of time.

I didn't feel deserving to be around upper echelon people or circumstances because I was still that shattered little girl deep down on the inside.

I don't like how you feel insecure at times.

I don't like when you feel you will always be abandoned, that nobody will ever stay.

- You get the point…

Please know there is no "formal" way to tell yourself what you don't like, or even regret about yourself and things you may have done. This list of Rights and Lefts are so very important. Do not feel bad for what you feel. It is not about "justifying" things in the now, it is about addressing things to let them go. It's about being honest and truthful with things that you may have never wanted to say out loud. I know this one may be tough because you may have some things you are not so proud of on this list, but be kind and loving to yourself. You are amazing and what you have been through and done, do NOT define you, or limit where you have yet to go. Maybe you have done the unthinkable. Maybe you have physically hurt someone or worse. Whatever it is, write it down. It's time to let it go. It's time to be free. The beautiful part about this work is that it's about you and you. You don't have to tell anyone if that is what you choose. You can do this! I believe in you! You're worth it!

Now we are Ready to journey into the next step, but before we do, I just want to remind you, **every step is powerful**, so please take your time with each step.

Step 3: Write it out!

Now that you have your T in order and you have created your right and left sides of the T, it is time to talk (write) it out! I say talk it out because I want you to imagine you are saying these things to the person on the T in real time. As if they are sitting across from you openly listening with no emotion or rebuttal, but with acceptance. That they WANT to hear what you have to say. Are you ready? <u>Please use the **EXACT** verbiage for the end of the letter that I will provide you with.</u>

First thing is to get a fresh piece of paper, write the person's name on the top, just like you would if you were writing a casual letter.

Dear________, then in the body of the letter take all the information you have on your T, and transfer it onto the new sheet paper in letter form.

You will find that more will come up as you do this. Please do NOT skip this step! Yes you have done the work with the T, but the letter is a part of the process. They serve two different purposes. **Yes, it's a lot of writing, but it's also a lot of baggage, so let's get rid of it!**

As you begin to write the letter you may find it harder than doing the T. You may find that tears are all you have for a minute or hours. **<u>You may find the biggest breakthrough in the first line of this letter.</u>** Each person will experience something different, but you will find there is something different about when you take what is on the T, and put it into a letter. **<u>As you write, be open, honest, transparent, and CRY, FEEL, and LET IT GO.</u>**

Use as many pages of paper as you need. My longest letter was 8 pages and the T that went with it was very small. <u>The letter brings something else to the table. Honor it.</u> **You will not be giving or showing anyone this letter, so don't hold back.**

Once you have written the letter, and you feel you are done, please follow the next direction to a T, no pun intended. Ok, maybe just a little. Ok, back to the seriousness, once all is written, write these words to finish the letter.

<u>I forgive you, and I send you love and light.</u> Write it word for word.

Then sign your name.

Step 4: The burn

Ok, so now you have a paperstack right? You have a T, and a letter? Good, now we are going to let it all go. I am sure at this point you are more than ready to say goodbye to all this baggage for good. Amen! I was too! Whew! It was a dark, long, emotional ride getting each and every T out. Remember you are not supposed to complete all T's at once, <u>you are supposed to go step by step and one by one.</u>

So at the point of burning, you should be burning one T, one letter. You should not have started one until you have given yourself sufficient time to finish it within 24 hours. In some instances you can handle a T a week, and with some T's you may need longer spurts between each one as some are harder than others. Honor yourself, this is NOT something to be taken lightly or RUSHED. This is serious work. So back to the burning process. I am sure some of you are standing with the matches just waiting for me to stop rambling. Ok, let me get to it. Last but not least before the instructions, here is my own personal disclaimer for any or all liability. **I am not responsible for irresponsible burning, or any injuries.** Please burn carefully and responsibly in a safe and containable situation. I have had some clients do it directly over a toilet or a sink so water is readily available. Ok, now that we have addressed that, lets talk about this burning.

Take all of your papers for that T and take it to where you will safely light it, burn it, and say, "IT IS DONE." There is something wonderful about watching the paper burn into ashes. As it burns, you are removing toxicity from your being and restoring it with love. I am proud of you, and you should be too.

During the burn, or once it is done, **<u>take a picture of it</u>**. I will explain why in the next step. **Congratulations**, you have just participated in some of the hardest work you will ever do in your life. You will feel a sense of **freedom** within. You will have such a <u>profound sense of love</u> for yourself like never before. You, my friend, have just **revived a part of you that was suffocating**. <u>You are amazing!</u> You are worth it! You always have been. One step to go!

Step 5: The Seal (The picture)

I am so proud of you! I know it was not easy. I am sure you experienced parts of yourself you didn't know were in there. You may have used more Kleenex than you have ever used in your life, but I know you know it was all worth it!

This last part that I call the **seal**, is simply that. You will take a picture of the burn, and you will send it to someone you love and trust without explanation. With clients they send it to me of course because I know what it is. When you share this with someone you are saying it is done, and here is the seal. **That this situation no longer has access to you**, it is sealed off. If you have someone in your life that knows you are doing this work, they are who you should be sending it to. This also gives them a chance to **celebrate** with you.

I always see the seal as a reminder of the scripture Matthew 18:20 "When two or more are gathered together in my name, I am in the midst of them" I fully believe that. **My God is love, and yes, love is in the midst of this work.**

CHAPTER 6

THE PURPOSE

In conclusion

My intention for this book was to provide anyone and everyone an opportunity to awaken, and restore themselves to their truest self. To live free and clear of past turmoil. To allow room for clarity, inspiration, and growth. To fully live a life free of dark and painful past experiences.

Not all people want to go and get help. They feel it is beneath them. Some can't afford it, or may not know where to get to it. For some people, they are willing to get help but have no clue what type of help or therapist, counselor, mentor, or coach they may need.

I hesitated writing this book because of the power behind it. I know deep diving into shadows within ourselves is not something all people have the strength to do alone. So I was bothered by the fact someone may get this book, and feel alone and terrified as they go through their T's alone. Then I was reminded, there are people that will only do this work if they are alone to do it. I know that there are some people that will never make that first call for help.

In the decision to go forward with writing this book, I was comforted by God knowing- he makes no mistakes with planting seeds. He grows the perfect garden. When he plants a vision, or a purpose, within you, it is with perfect alignment with his will. We are not to be the judgment behind the gifts he gives, we are to be the givers of the gifts he gives. So needless to say, here is the book.

Now that you have all this loving and free space within you, it is time to cultivate yourself for your best self. This means cultivating healthy daily practices. Such as eating right, sleeping well, reading, goal and vision planning, having fun, making time for yourself, and continuing to walk in a positive direction.

You will find that throughout life you will find opportunities to use this process. Out of the blue something may cause an emotional jolt within you and you will say "aha, I need to do a T on that/him/her." This is called awareness my friends. T's aren't just for people but also for subjects such as abortions, drug abuse, adoptions, alcoholism, and other "matters" that need to be processed. Keep this book, go step by step, please do not skip things. Be thorough. Now go back to the "the list" part and go to work!

I believe in you, and I am excited for the new found joy you will experience from doing this exercise. Your happiness adds to my happiness, as we are all one drop in this big ocean we call life. We are all universally connected, and the sooner we get that, the better we will be for it. May you live a blessed life as you liberate yourself from the survival emotions you were once bound by. I send you love and light, be sure to tell yourself at least 2 times a day, " I CAN, I WILL, I AM WORTH IT!"

I send you all love and light,
Lady B.

ABOUT THE AUTHOR

Amy L. Bolding "Lady B" was born and raised in California. She currently resides in the states Georgia and New York. Prior to being the amazing light and love bearing soul she is today, she endured less than favorable circumstances. She was a 4 pound baby born to a drug using mother, who passed away when she was the tender age of 6. She experienced foster care, and was moved home to home throughout her younger years. During that time she was what the system called a high risk youth, she ran away multiple times trying to avoid the abuse she was enduring while being in these places. She had even slept outside to avoid the pain of abuse. She had encountered multiple sexual abuse encounters by family members and foster living situations. She eventually went on to live on her own when she was 17. Unfortunately she went from an abusive childhood, to an abusive relationship which one instance led her to not even being able to recognize her own face and being locked in a closet. It didn't end there. On two separate occasions she was involved in a wreck with a 18 wheeler and walked away with minor damage. Talk about a survivor! She was a high school drop out, but went on to eventually get her GED and on to college. She raised 3 wonderful children single handedly, and became a Nurse. It seemed like everything was starting to turn around for her, when the floor as she knew it fell out from under her yet again. She was a victim of excessive force by the police in front of her children. Where her and her youngest son sustained injuries, and the pain sustained as they went through a 2 year court battle. She would have never imagined at 40 years old life would hit her with such a twist. A time so hard it had her digging in the dumpster for survival. How does this happen? The next plot twist- she earns an IMdB credit for acting in a short film. She started The Bold Movement, she trademarked the slogan, "I CAN, I WILL, I'M WORTH IT!" and got in the best shape of her life. Things seemed to be on an upward swing, then just when she felt that she was confident in her new place of inspiration and healing, her best friend committed suicide. Needless to say, the silver spoon wasn't at the table. She had a lot of pain, endurance, perseverance, and determination. She teaches from being the student, a place that is genuine. How does that happen? And what led her to be a dumpster diver? And how do you just go into acting out of nowhere with no experience? Inquiring minds want to know, right? Well, let's just talk about some of that briefly, and we will save the rest for the interviews. The pivotal moment for her was when she decided there has to be more to life than what she was experiencing. She decided this was either where she quits, or puts her foot on the gas pedal into recreating her life. She went into what has now been over a 6 year journey of learning how to live a life of awareness. As explained in the first part of this book, it wasn't a cakewalk, and it required a ton of courage and commitment to healing and creating a new reality. There was a LOT of unknown she had to be willing to walk into. Amy was mentored by Les Brown, spoke on his virtual stage, and is a certified power voice speaker through his program. It was like a dream come true for her as she speaks of the times it was the voice of zig ziglar and Les Brown that would keep her going at times. Becoming a student of Les Brown was such an honor for her. She is a heavy follower and student of the following gifted souls: Dr. Wayne Dyer, Thich Nhat Hanh, Dr. Joe Dispenza, Abraham Hicks, Florence Scovel Shinn, Napoleon Hill, Louise Hay, Pema Chodron, Rumi, Paramahansa Yogananda, Les Brown, Bob Proctor, Zig Ziglar, Michael Bernard Beckwith, Neville Goddard, Michael Singer, Gary Zukov, Yung Pueblo, Buddha, Jesus Christ, God himself.

Lady B. is a speaker, author, and awareness coach who offers a unique insight paired with proven techniques to her clients. She focuses on helping clients with mind and body awareness and healing. Her typical client has endured tumultuous circumstances in their life primarily during their younger years. These clients feel stuck, hopeless, and at times flat out angry with life. As an awareness coach she benefits her clients with her medical background and personal life experiences. She is a Les Brown certified speaker and speaks around the globe. She is a former student of the Bob Proctor program, "Thinking Into Results." In 2021 participated in a Tony Robbins endorsed book titled "Cracking the Rich Code" she was a featured author in Vol. 6. She was also a contributing author in the book, "Cultivating your Mindset for Success" with her piece titled "Trusting and Becoming." Lady B. is the founder of The Pickled Heart LLC. Where she continues to expand The Bold Movement to be a global impact of self-awareness, self-love, healing, and transformation. She currently provides group T therapy, individual T therapy, one and one awareness coaching, motivational bootcamps, and keynote speaking.

Her mission is to infuse love, hope, and courage into the world one person at a time with her work. To teach, heal, and be the light God called her to be.

If you are interested in her services her contact information is below.

Amy L. Bolding (Lady B.)
The Pickled Heart LLC
Thepickledheart@gmail.com
(619) 770-9847

www.ingramcontent.com/pod-product-compliance
Lightning Source LLC
Chambersburg PA
CBHW021142130726
47988CB00003B/1427